Pebble® Plus

Science Builders

Soil Basics

by Mari Schuh

Consulting Editor: Gail Saunders-Smith, PhD

Consultant: Joanne K. Olson, PhD
Associate Professor, Science Education
Center for Excellence in Science & Mathematics Education
Iowa State University, Ames

CAPSTONE PRESS
a capstone imprint

Pebble Plus is published by Capstone Press,
151 Good Counsel Drive, P.O. Box 669, Mankato, Minnesota 56002.
www.capstonepub.com

Books published by Capstone Press are manufactured with paper
containing at least 10 percent post-consumer waste.

Library of Congress Cataloging-in-Publication Data
Schuh, Mari C., 1975–
  Soil basics / by Mari Schuh.
    p. cm.—(Pebble plus. Science builders)
  Includes bibliographical references and index.
  Summary: "Simple text and full-color photographs provide a brief introduction to soil"—Provided by publisher.
  ISBN 978-1-4296-6071-6 (library binding)
  ISBN 978-1-4296-7110-1 (paperback)
  1. Soils—Juvenile literature. I. Title.
  S591.3S38 2012
  631.4—dc22   2010053935

Editorial Credits
Erika L. Shores, editor; Bobbie Nuytten and Ashlee Suker, designers; Wanda Winch, media researcher;
    Laura Manthe, production specialist

Photo Credits
Getty Images Inc.: Visuals Unlimited/NSIL/G.R. "Dick" Roberts, 11, 15, 22-23; iStockphoto Inc.: Marcin Pawinski,
17, Oksana Tumeniuk-Malashenko, 13, Paul Roux, 9, Susan H. Smith, 7; Shutterstock: Barbro Bergfeldt, 19, Elena
Moiseeva, 21, Liliya Kulianionak, 5, Nina Malyna, cover, NitroCephal, 1

Note to Parents and Teachers

The Science Builders series supports national science standards related to earth science.
This book describes and illustrates soil. The images support early readers in understanding
the text. The repetition of words and phrases helps early readers learn new words. This book
also introduces early readers to subject-specific vocabulary words, which are defined in the
Glossary section. Early readers may need assistance to read some words and to use the Table of
Contents, Glossary, Read More, Internet Sites, and Index sections of the book.

Printed in the United States of America in North Mankato, Minnesota.
032011   006110CGF11

Table of Contents

What Is Soil?

Flowers sprout in soil. Soil helps vegetables grow big and ripe. Soil covers most of Earth's land.

Soil is made from rocks
and rotting plants and animals.
Soil also holds water and air.

7

Soil forms as rocks
break down into tiny pieces.
Bits of sand, silt, and clay
are in soil.

Soil's Layers

Dig a hole and you'll see
that soil forms in layers.
Plants grow in the top layer
called topsoil.

Topsoil is rich in humus.

Humus is dark, moist,

and full of nutrients.

Humus is made of rotting

plants and animals.

Under the topsoil is a layer

called subsoil.

Subsoil has less humus

and is not as loose as topsoil.

Subsoil is often filled with clay.

Healthy Soil

All sorts of creatures keep soil healthy. Moles tunnel through soil. By loosening soil, moles help plant roots have room to grow.

Plants need nutrients to grow.

Bacteria break down rotting plants

and animals into soil nutrients.

Earthworms add nutrients to soil

with their droppings.

Look at a plant.

Find a worm.

Follow a mole hole.

Healthy soil is full of life.

Glossary

bacteria—very small organisms that exist inside and around all living things

clay—a kind of soil that can be shaped when wet; clay feels hard when it is dry; clay particles are small

humus—a dark, rich material full of nutrients from rotting plants and animals

nutrient—a substance needed by a living thing to stay healthy

rot—to decay or break down

silt—a kind of particle found in soil; silt particles are bigger than clay, but smaller than sand; silt feels powdery

Read More

Aloian, Molly. *Different Kinds of Soil.* Everybody Digs Soil. New York: Crabtree Pub., 2009.

Faulkner, Rebecca. *Soil.* Geology Rocks! Chicago: Raintree, 2007.

Green, Jen. *Rocks and Soil.* Our Earth. New York: PowerKids Press, 2008.

Guillain, Charlotte. *Rocks and Soil.* Investigate. Chicago: Heinemann Library, 2008.

Internet Sites

FactHound offers a safe, fun way to find Internet sites related to this book. All of the sites on FactHound have been researched by our staff.

Here's all you do:

Visit *www.facthound.com*

Type in this code: 9781429660716

Check out projects, games and lots more at
www.capstonekids.com

23

Index

Word Count: 178
Grade: 1
Early-Intervention Level: 20